Sudden Hunger

Also by Debra Bruce

Pure Daughter

Sudden Hunger

poems by Debra Bruce

The University of Arkansas Press

Fayetteville   1987

Designer: Chiquita Babb
Typeface: Linotron 202 Perpetua
Typesetter: G & S Typesetters, Inc.
Printer: Thomson-Shore, Inc.
Binder: John H. Dekker & Sons, Inc.

The paper used in this publication meets the minimum requirements of the
American National Standard for Permanence of Paper for Printed Library
Materials Z39.48-1984. ∞

Grateful acknowledgment is made to the following publications in which many of
these poems, sometimes in earlier versions, appeared:

*Amaryllis Review, The American Poetry Review, Anthology of Magazine Verse & Yearbook of
American Poetry (Monitor Books), Calyx, Frontiers, The Massachusetts Review, Mississippi Re-
view, Negative Capability, Open Places, Passages North, Poetry Northwest, Prairie Schooner,* and
Virginia Quarterly Review.

I would like to thank the Illinois Arts Council and Northeastern Illinois University
for grants that helped me to complete this book.

Library of Congress Cataloging-in-Publication Data

Bruce, Debra, 1951–
    Sudden hunger.
    I. Title.
PS3552.R7918S8   1987   811'.54   86-16091
ISBN 0-938626-81-7
ISBN 0-938626-82-5 (pbk.)

For Joan and Fred Silva

Contents

III

IV

Sudden Hunger

I

Athenian Wife Waiting For Her Husband

5th century B.C.

Damp cheese crumbles on my fingers.
I lick it slowly, let myself linger
here alone. I've had them cook the fish
the way I know he likes it, the best bite,
that muscle of cheek still moist and tight
for him. For him. But where is he now
at dusk? Cupping his wine cup, sipping
with his men, smiling at them, nipping
a bit of leek, a puckered olive tucked
beneath his tongue? How I would love to hear
his words as he puts his lips to the ear
of another man. Or is it some boy again,
a shapely mouth, a blond head that blinds
him with love each month or so? Do I mind?
I try not to think. I rub a red root
in circles on my cheeks and wait for his thighs,
those runner's thighs to bring him back. I sigh
and hold my own hands. They're cool and closed.
I want him to come here and open them,
lift up my beaded, belted robes, and then
forget that boy he kissed an hour ago,
who made the honeyed hills of Athens hum,
who held my husband's body so hard the sun
rushed into his head
and burned me away—woman,
wife, bed.

The Centauress

The Rodin Museum, Philadelphia

All around me, women melt
into their lovers, inside the hot
hand of god, or down to the lips
of a tugging boy, to suckle him
with a kiss. Women ripen
inward, alone,
crouching low, closing their eyes,
letting their fingers find,
lowering slowly, their own breasts.
I will never rest
in this body. I hear the young
men's muscles breathing in bronze.
An athlete sits, his thighs open,
a length of leg to run my tongue along.
In another room a woman
lets her hair pour down
her bare back, her lover's mouth
wandering past her mound
of belly, his hands held
behind his back. Don't tell me
it wouldn't be better
like that, my wet
legs letting me go,
my body learning slowly
to straddle human hips.

4

For Roxeanna in Spring

You make me think of petals opening wide,
ambrosia-tulips burning at their tips.
Desire is not something we decide.

It's something planted in us, deep inside,
before we notice men's or women's hips.
You make me think of petals opening wide,

filling with sun. All spring I try to hide
by answering your questions with a quip.
Desire is not something we decide.

It spills up from our roots. I stand beside
such purple hyacinths I want to sip
on one, taste petals open wide.

Pressure blooms in my mouth. I want to confide
in you. I have never kissed your lips.
Desire is not something we decide.

I love to watch wisteria split the sides
of phallic sacs and bloom, but I must not slip,
admit my love while petals open wide.
Desire is not something we decide.

Sonnet MVI

Since you love her, I know you'll understand
that when I met her, you-know-whose hot dart
hit me and hurt. Although I'm not a man.
Love's not determined by who has what part.
If it were, then how could I have felt this?
The steamy mirror, her robe on the floor . . .
She soaped slow circles over her pelvis
as I watched her through the blurry shower door.
If I loved her, I'd only verify
what you know well. The thought heats up my hips.
I'm jealous of your cheek on her thigh
as she holds your hair, rides against your lips.
If she loved me, she'd understand what you
love so much about her. What I love too.

Navy Town Spring

A big-bellied bouncer bangs
the door open wide and leans
on it and lights up in the sun.

Inside, the deep dark bar
begins to breathe, tickling
a sailor's neck until he lifts

his head from the table and squints.
The bar is sticky, barstools licked
by sunlight. Men taste

noon on their tongues and hold up
their hands and groan.

Lou's Tattoo has its door open too.
A chain, a heart, a mermaid
on your arm forever.

The young ones swagger out
into the sun, their shirts off, tied
around their waists, their jeans too tight.

In every bar on Ocean View,
tonight is Ladies' Night.

Navy Town Weekend

At midnight his Trans Am is off
the road on the wrong side,
lip to lip with a cop car.

The green-eyed girl he keeps
tattooed on his arm looks up
at two cops looking down at him,

his head flung back in sleep.
Today he found a spot on the beach
and lay there, watching gold girls,

sculpted girls who didn't know him.
He saw the ocean sliding toward them,
slide over, under their feet.

He knows some sailors who spit
the name of this place, Shit City,
though honeysuckle grows around

the bar where he drank at noon,
at dusk. Remembering the sweetness
of it, he nipped one flower,

and sipped. All these hours
his submarine has been waiting
under humpbacked water, its belly

already heavy with boys like him.

Navy Pilot

1

His jacket's a leather-chested swagger
he slips on with a smile,
as snug and sleek as a mink
on a sexy woman on his arm.

A dozen like him have died this year.
He drinks another drink.

2

Below him
is the town where his children
sit down at their desks all day
like other children, their voices
held down by a teacher's voice.
But their father can break the rules:
when his F-14 screams, the teacher holds
her hands in the air and waits
while their father flies over the school.

3

He says he's not the type to die
like the others.
He knows how to fall in a ball
of himself, safe in the enemy woods.
He says he can sleep
in a tree, he can slit
the skins of lizards in the dark
and eat them—without a sizzle,
without a spark.

4

The pilot's wife waits.
Waits. When he comes back
they'll shuck some rough-backed oysters
on the beach, let a kettle of shrimp
shudder to a blush, then crush
the shells off softly in their hands
and eat until they can't get up,
until he lies back on his bare back
and his youngest boys come running,
barefoot, to bury him in the sand,
in the sun.

After Dinner,
She Discusses Marriage with Her Friends

I'll never forget the first time I slept
with him. He told me things I almost wept
to hear—how he'd slip out at dawn as a boy
to pick loamy mushrooms in a field. Joy
flowed through him as he simmered them in cream
while his parents slept. I thought I was dreaming
that next morning when I wobbled out of bed,
thinking he was gone, finding him, instead,
looking down at my skillet, my two white plates.
He watched frying eggs slowly undulate.
Corn bread was in the oven, peach preserves
in a dish. What had I done to deserve
a lover like this? Soon after breakfast
I phoned a justice of the peace. The rest
is history. Friends laugh when we tell them.
Then their smiles weaken and fade away. Then
their faces go blank and they look at us
as if we're morons waving from a bus
at strangers. I know what they want to know.
They think there's got to be more. Food can go
but so far to explain the mystery
of human intimacy. I agree.
But there's always one more secret to share:
this same boy picked raspberries, hiding there,
the ripe and soft-lipped fruit pressed to his own
soft lips at dusk as his parents called him home.

I taste that memory and hunger more
for him. Our friends start glancing at the door,
the window, anything but us, confused,
as if they'd asked for coffee and been refused.
I hear him in the kitchen. Now he comes
with cups of apple compote soaked in rum.
Conversation resumes. Somebody asks
about monogamy. How can it last?
He pours my mocha java. How many times
I've sat on the porch alone while my mind
simmered with lust, watching our landlord's son
clipping geraniums. Fresh cardamom
drifting from the kitchen couldn't compete
with those gold shoulders, those naked, shapely feet.
I've straddled the railing, wanting, for hours,
to ride him bareback into the flowers,
letting myself fall slowly, slowly off
and spill beneath him, his voice as soft
as strokes of butter melting on warm bread.
Of course I've never done this, as I said.
But I've come close. One summer day I reached
for that boy's black hair. Suddenly the screech
of the screen door—My husband! He'll clobber
us both! But he'd brought blueberry cobbler
for me, and a tart whose fan of sliced pears
was draped in silky chocolate everywhere.

Tasting the tart from his finger, I learned
such depths of chocolate, a sweetness so stern
I couldn't even moan. Now, not a word
is spoken. My friends stare as if they'd heard
me say I took a linzer torte to bed
or slept with upside-down cake at my head.
They shake their heads, my husband's hand, and go.
It's late but I'll stay up, watch him make dough
for breakfast biscuits, grind up cinnamon,
melt down butter and knead the raisins in.
He'll bake them in the morning, plump and sweet,
sugared together on a baking sheet.

II

Young Wife Waiting for the Results of Her Husband's Biopsy

1

She crushes a paper coffee cup
in her lap. (This can't be happening.)
Nurses murmur. (She remembers her grandmother's
shadow murmuring, shades drawn, a rosary
rolling over her hands.) A thousand miles away
from this bright place, her parents, his parents
wait for her call. She tugged the cord
as she told them. Just last week
she ground up fresh French roast at home
with him, stirring
a cinnamon stick in. Its tight scroll
unraveled on their tongues, its taste unrolled.

2

This morning she smelled the cut
grass blowing past
the man next door as he mowed his lawn.
He has lived there so long.
At noon his wife will shake moist lettuce
in the shade and call him
into that cool place.

3

The hospital towers. A summer holly
flowers, a veil of bees hovering
above it. (She remembers summer Sundays,
her mother making her pin her veil
down, pin down the heat that rose
and fell on her head as she walked to church.
The thick-tongued bells she used to believe
told her she would always come, come.)

4

Someone calls her name.
The doctor says her husband
does not have, her husband will live . . .
is the answer.

5

Her husband sleeps. Hunger
eats her so suddenly she must go
home to tear up bread, eat olives, peppers,
palm hearts, cheese, drink dark beer.
The humid windows in her house are stuck
shut. She shoves them open.

Out there
a rosebush flaps. The couple next door
pack up their lunch and go inside
because the sky is getting dark.
She opens her door. Wind
wraps, unwraps her clothes.
The sky is dark. The wind picks up and blows
around her porch some scraps of rose.

The Admiral's Wife

She's flying tonight from somewhere
to somewhere, having packed two years
of a German town into trunks and fastened
every lock. Then Lisbon, Madrid, slips
of oily eel in paella she couldn't eat,
the street in Paris where the ambassador
was shot as he lifted his hand to cough,
walking to his car. Her husband
is beside her as the plane takes off,
but the world keeps spinning below them,
out of reach. A slim young terrorist
her own son's age is somewhere, dozing
on a terrace. Mahogany conference rooms
keep disappearing in the smoky breath
of important men who cannot find him.
Her husband puts his damp forehead
on her shoulder and sleeps. She stays awake,
remembering his first long cruise,
how the humid hours oozed by her in the small
house all summer by a ship-grey sea,
how he came home with silk that stroked
her wrists, with paintings of soft, draped
mountains he'd seen in Asia.

By now she's seen her own face change
and soften in oval mirrors
in Gaeta, London, in the hours
after the elegant luncheons,
after all the wives, the ladies, the women
were gone.
Below the clouds her children's children
sleep in another country while she travels
back through time to meet them,
to memorize each face before she leaves
for another house, another base,
where cool rain will drill into a beach,
and a warm breeze finally feather
the air with salt. Now she must
make herself at home among this cargo
of guns, Belgian chocolates, wine.
Now she must fly like this
all night.

Mother and Daughter

She yanks the burgundy dress off the rack,
shoves it at her mother. Her eyes are wet,
her hand bumps mine. What was wrong with the black
one over there? Why can't her mother let
her shop alone? Why can't her mother go?
Mother's love is pulled over her shoulders:
she twists herself to jab through it, there's no
way to breathe. It squeezes her hips, holds her.

Her mother is watching in the mirror
under the bright bulb. When she leaves, the girl
is alone, so close to me I can hear her
still breathing hard. So many dresses swirl
under her hand as she pushes them, hits
the empty hangers. Nothing. Nothing fits.

Father, Son, Grandson

Your father tosses your baby toward the sun.
They both laugh. Their faces glisten.
You watch, listen, as if that's what you've come
back to do. The red-faced father you knew
leaned across your math book after supper,
flicked his pencil inches from your face,
hissed your name as he snapped it in two.

Now your father's summer garden blooms
around you. He kneels there
with his grandson, stroking the round,
ripe shapes he names so slowly:
cantaloupe, eggplant. Those hands
that used to twitch toward his belt
until you ran and ran.
Who is this man who takes the time
to touch inside a flower? A shower
of pollen powders his fingertips.
He brushes his lips across his grandson's cheek.

You watch from under a tree,
too far away for your father to see
the first wisp of skin just slipping
loose from your neck, though your back
is straight as a boy's. It tastes
so bitter—this grass you've plucked up
to break a blade on your teeth and tongue

and give a whistle so sharp
they both look at you and wave:
first your father, then your son.

My Father Refuses to Read the Obituaries

His sisters are furious. Doesn't he want to know
about his old buddies when they go? Aunt Grace throws
the folded paper into his lap, drops her purse
on the couch, leans on the arm of his chair. This perverse
old brother of hers winks up, smiling, slowly tears
the paper in two. How dare
he do it?—she shrieks—
She's carried that folded obit page for weeks,
knowing he never gets *The Burnt Hills Daily.*
You old fool, Billy—his first paper wad comes sailing
across the book I'm trying to read, just misses me.
Grace bends her bad back, yanks out the plug by the Christmas tree

and leaves us there. Aunt Ellen's shadow is pulling bobby pins
from her hair, holding them in her teeth. *You have to win,*
don't you, Billy? Her hair unwound, then winding back
up again, the pins pushed in. Her curses crackle
softly as she leaves. Here comes my youngest sister
to perch next to me, whisper,
Now what did Daddy do?
I turn on the tree and show her the page he threw
in there. I hear dry needles tick on unopened gifts
as I crawl in. Daddy snores. My sister giggles. I lift
it out. She breathes warm gusts of booze on me, pops
open a beer. We smooth the crumpled names across our laps,
but it's time to eat. Daddy twitches awake at the call

of women through the wall. We squeeze in on chairs, stools, all
thirteen of us. Daddy's face is as pink as the ham
he's about to slice. But first he grabs my mother's hand,
commanding, *Say grace, dearie,* and smirks right through her prayer.
She crosses herself. Everyone there
is thinking about his soul
as he sharpens his carving knife, squints down at a bowl
of yams, then dozes off. My mother nudges him. His cheeks
are bright with sweat. Everyone is watching. No one speaks
until he opens his eyes, belches, then winks at Aunt Grace
who slams down her spoon, *This is my last Christmas at this place!*

But she doesn't mean it. Daddy knows she doesn't. He shakes
his head at her when he hears his grandson shriek awake,
Look what you've done, Grace. The baby's carried in, his face
knotted tight. Daddy applauds, holds out his arms. A lace
of slow snow is filling the window as he holds him and keeps
on rocking him slowly, humming
low, his voice coming
from farther and farther away. Now the baby's breathing deep
down the diamond-crossed lines in Daddy's neck. Now he will sleep.

Aunt Judith and Her Housemate, Ann

Don't say they are in love
with each other. What
would the mint-scented nephew think
who reaches down to kiss
his girl under the mistletoe?
Now he hugs Aunt Judith,
hello to the housemate, he pumps
her soft hand hard.
Judith and Ann stand far apart.
They do not bend to slip
each other's boots off, brush
soft bits of snow
from each other's coats.

What would the little ones think
who run barefoot over scraps
of wrapping paper to jump
into Aunt Judith's arms,
Scotch tape stuck to their feet?
Or Judith's niece who nurses
her newest one in a chair
by the Christmas tree, hums
into its first whisper of hair?
Judith and Ann have been good friends
for fifteen years. Don't say
couple. They will not

crumple together on this couch,
mouth to mouth. Ann sits here.

Judith sits there.
The smallest children climb them.
Someone's boy play-punches
the pillow of Ann's belly.
Someone's girl breathes softly
against Judith's cheek, lays
a strand of tinsel on Judith's hair.

For Roxeanna in Summer

You have to tell me all
about his June bronze back,
the chiseled line of his hips,
tiger lilies leaping at the window
above your bed, his hand reaching
over your head to pick one
after rain and drag its damp
petals across your lips.

You tell me when women kiss
women, love women, something
is missing. Am I listening?
I pull the cutting board closer
and listen. I bruise rosemary, mint,
crush hot red pepper carefully.
This cruet of virgin oil almost
slips from my fingers in its first
green gush. Can't I imagine
your lust for such a man? You touch
my mouth, put an olive on my tongue.
Yes. I can.

Reading Your Book on the Beach,
Many Years Later

My mouth is full of mint
and ice as I drink you in.
Read you, I mean. I've learned
to tell a woman from her words.
These long-legged lines cannot
be you, but lying on this hot
sand I remember how you'd stand
by a window—leggy, tense, tan.
I smell strawberries, sliced apple
on a summer page. I see you nibble
each one, your sheer shirt blown
against you. I should have outgrown
all this, but even now
I hear you laugh, showing us how
your lover tongued fruit. A joke
in a roomful of women. We never spoke
of him again, that lover who
lies undulant underneath you
on a beach, in a bed, all summer
in this book. I was younger
than you. I reached out to take it
from your hand—the beaded blackberry—break it
against my lips.

My Mother Refuses to Tell Her Age

Here comes my mother, flying overhead
in her new boyfriend's plane. I haven't met
him yet. I don't know if her hair is red

this summer or gold. I wait below and frown,
my thick legs standing firmly on the ground,
murmuring to myself, *Mother, come down*

from there right now. When her hips come swinging in,
the airport lounge buzzes bright. She grins
and waves a jewelled hand. Who'd think we're kin?

I'm a blonde but bland as a peeled potato.
I've worn thick glasses since I was one-day-old.
I married a skinny man with a halo

around his head. That's what my mother thinks.
She'd like to rumple it up, fix him a drink,
see what he has to say. But he just blinks

incredulously as she sashays toward
us now, followed by the boyfriend, forty
or so years old. I just turned thirty-four,

which brings me to the subject of her age.
But wait—her name is called. She's being paged
to the airport phone. Her other beau, enraged

to find her gone, somehow managed to learn
her destination. Does he know she's spurned
his love for this one here? My face burns

as I look at him. I would rather be dead,
but I heave a smile, inquire mildly instead,
Ever been here before? He nods his head.

But getting back to her age. This boyfriend here
is no doubt misinformed about her years.
I lean toward my husband, my lips to his ear,

while boyfriend, watching, thinks I'm about to kiss
him sweetly. I smile back at boyfriend, hiss
at husband, *She can't drag me into this!*

Here she comes, earrings swinging. On the spot
I swoop up her bags, tell her, *Wait here, it's hot.*
I go galumphing across the parking lot.

One spring I met her surgeon, Dr. Older.
(I did not make up this name.) I told her
she must tell him the truth. She rolled her

shadowed blue eyes. What difference could it make?
After her operation, her hands were shaky
as I held them. Her face looked so naked

without makeup. She looked her age: fifty-two.
I stroked her wrists, wondering if she knew
I was afraid. I didn't know what to do

but watch the monitor light up each time
her heart beat. That's when I saw the sign:
Mary Bruce, Age: 39.

I remember I wanted to slaughter
her then and there. She looked at me and winked.
I will never understand why I winked
at her and smiled—her raging, wrinkling daughter.

III

Mid-life Crisis

Your shaved-off beard peppers the bathroom sink
with the old you. In the mirror, that pale boy's chin,
like a smoothed-down oval of soap, makes you grin
back at him. I wonder what he thinks
of you, the skinny stairs that lead to your door,
the sweet white wine you pour like water
into a mug for a girl young as your daughter
who sits on a mattress on the floor.

Somewhere under October trees, the white,
two-story house you left behind still stands.
Your wife, ex-wife, will never understand.
When you told her you couldn't breathe, the tight
sky split apart. Wind tumbled down the eaves,
letting loose a spicy whisper of leaves.

Aging Mother at the Health Club

At sixty I am supposed to start melting
down to a creamy dollop of flesh
in clouds of perfumed powder for my daughters'
daughters to taste as they kiss my face
and grimace and turn away.

I am supposed to huddle against closed
doors, listening to my girls laugh
over a list of past lovers, praising
this one, that one, the salt-lick belly
of the smoothest blond.

I should hunch in closets
digging forever through crammed
cardboard boxes for something I must
have forgotten or lost.
Once there was a pond

where I let my daughters skate
as late as they wanted over moonlit
patterns of trapped twigs.
I rubbed their limp legs dry
when they came inside.

Now all I want is to move
in my body in this exercise room,
to follow the shapely movements
of a younger woman. At home
I'll find one daughter waiting

to visit me, waiting to go,
to hoist her youngest and wave
its hand goodbye to Grandma.
I've seen that daughter smile down
at me, shake her head

at my neckline's low-cut curve
and I've wanted to press her hand
there, make her feel how hard
my heart beats, beats, without a skip.
I've wanted to pull her mouth toward mine
and kiss that smirk from her lips.

The Last Time I Saw Her

My mother crushed a ten-dollar bill
into my hand. I pushed it back.
The bag of pecan-rolls, stollen,
cinnamon swirls was crumpled
between us, spreading its sticky
sweet stain.

I was driving her to a morning train
that would take her home. The hot
haze that hung over her visit
was gone. A cool sky broke through.
We rode with the windows down.
We hardly spoke.

I touched her shoulder, then let her go
into the shadow of the train.
I held my arms at my side.
The birds she loved were loud
with early morning. The birds shrieked,
gabbled, cried, wake up, too late, goodbye.

Never Married

I've never asked them, those two aunts of mine.
My mother, when I asked, looked up and sighed
as if she'd opened a door, hoping to find
them there, but didn't, as if they might hide
somewhere. But I remember sitting between
them on the porch while they both stroked my hair.
Summer sagged breathlessly against the screen.
I slipped down in their smells. I slept in there.

Now I lean down to help them up the steps.
I want to say what I could never say,
as they hold me, kissing my ears, my neck.
I lift my head. It's wind that slaps my face.
I want to ask them once, before they go,
how they lived. That's all I want to know.

For Roxeanna in Fall

You call at midnight. I can't get back to sleep.
Into my lap the cat throws her heap of heat

and purrs so hard I almost think she knows
about you. I almost believe she'll go

and nuzzle my lover's beard, lick him awake
and tell him. I hear the kitchen door shake

in the wind. Last fall the apples were thrown
to the ground by now, and I'd grown

so close to you. Bees sagged in the sun,
following us, their heavy, honeyed hum

filling our heads. I waved them away, pulled
you into the shade. I tasted the mulled,

sweet pear you held to my mouth. When I bit
a plum, it startled my tongue with a spit

of wine, like a kiss I didn't expect.
I don't know exactly what happened next.

After you call I twist the cord into tight
knots in my lap. They won't come out. I bite

an apple so green, so hard it hurts my mouth.

The Clock in the Museum

In many museums, a cosmic clock illustrates the history of life
on earth, showing that human life begins a few minutes before
midnight.

Twilight and nobody
here, almost as if
we forgot, or God
forgot, letting the earth
roll, boil, the whole
day, licked by lava
and suddenly thinking to let
one worm ooze
loose from mud, then
a thump as the first snake
tightens its belly. The legs
of the grasshopper listen.
Nobody. Just the first
flower breaking open
one hour before
midnight. A ring-tailed lemur
spilling its musk slowly
into deep grooves of bark.
Now one tall
Iroquois squaw, her dark daughter
stripping silk from corn
in the shade. In just a few
minutes she will finish
her task, then sleep

deep in those woods. The bones
of her hands will be buried
under a birch and dug up
there, in my childhood.

The Restaurant Where We Lived

Fereydun and my father made a deal.
Our house is his now, his
black-eyed boys behind the bar
looking up as my sister and I step
into their cocktail lounge, our old front porch,
two ladies out to lunch.

Reservations in our living room.
The big bay window still full
of the willow my father planted out there.
My tree. Her tree. Mine. I pulled her
by the roots of her hair.
I bit her hot face.

Two place settings of silver, linen napkins
in our laps. Our parents' bedroom wall
knocked out behind me, candles lit
in that corner where now a couple
sits, smiling, their hands laced
on the white tablecloth, a bucket of wine.

My father's fist, his chair scraped back,
my mother's hands in her lap, the back door
slammed. Now they eat in separate kitchens,
separate houses, while here a young chef
sautés garlic, bleeds its sting away,
makes a sweet sauce and later swings

through his kitchen doors to ask,
How do we like it? How do we like the attic
of our house an elegant balcony where couples
share escargot? The army blanket where we buried
each other in smells, the corner eaves where bees
nested, hanging all winter in a changing

cluster, a fist of fur turning and turning
to stay alive. They did not survive
Fereydun. Nothing stings anyone
who dines here. That was childhood
and this is adulthood, this cool carafe
of wine, my sister's laugh-lines smiling

at me, and the willow tapping its delicate
straps against the window at her back.

My Father's Visits

You spot a loose nail on my porch and pound
it down so it won't snag me later when you
are gone. Hammer in hand, you prowl around
and around for something broken, something to do.
I think you think a father should only stay
to fix his daughter's house, then go away.

You jingle change in your pocket. Your coffee steams
the window where you stand and tell me how free
you feel since you retired. You spot one flame
of cardinal twitching. You explain how he
will survive this northern winter, burn back in May.
But when I look he fidgets, then flies away.

If you could stay just one more day I'd listen
to you describe the dawn, the racket of flak
as you flew over Italy, every mission.
Below you, unpicked olives gone gold, then black.
The details tumble into disarray.
Your bomber staggers. I watch it fly away.

I watch it fly away with you inside,
breathing fast, a young blond bombardier.
Your buddy, the navigator, hugs your waist, hides
behind you. Your neck is wet with his fear.
Your plane leaves here at six o'clock today.
I'll stand at the gate until it flies away.

I make you promise to come back in the spring.
Of course, you laugh, and slap your suitcase shut.
I'll never have time to ask you everything.
Sun on your skin in Corsica, the chestnut
shade where, finally, after raiding, you lay.
What did you dream there? I ask. You turn away.

IV

*L*ula Mae's Morning Swim

Imagine the water
in her lane stretching as far
as she's swum into one long strip
like cloth, scalloped by her strokes.
By now she could have drifted
to her girlhood in Savannah,
could have climbed up
into the porch swing, dripping
dusk and waiting
for her parents' shadows to go
upstairs, for a boy named Phil
who hid by the flowering quince
to meet her with the suitcase
down by the gate.

Now Phil waits at home,
eased into his chair while she
dries her gray hair in this locker room.
Since his second stroke, the house
they built together by hand
keeps dozing off. She wakes
each morning, fixes him ham-biscuits
and apple butter, puts his TV tray
in the den with pecan walls,
then walks a mile to swim
another mile. At seventy-five it feels

like nothing until she climbs out
of the water back into her body
and stretches on the deck. Then
she feels her own pounding,
demanding heart.

In Search of an Explanation

Her husband jumped from the plane
but someone else fell
out of the summer sky that day
in her husband's parachute, fell deep
into sleep for a week in her husband's
broken bones, woke up,
didn't know her.

The doctors' report said her husband,
thirty-five, survived.
The navy report agreed: alive.
She wheeled the stranger home.

Her children still back away
from the droop of his head, his wet loose lips.
Like big slow boys who try to talk
to them at school, he drags his voice
across the gravel vowels.

By winter she knows how
to lift him from the bed.
The counselor said, the priest said . . .
His body wanders in her arms
as she knots his robe. He smiles
into his lap, reaches down
to toss the bathrobe tassels this way
and that.

On Their Golden Anniversary, Granny Dunn Remembers Their First Northern Winter

I saw you smiling down at slush, thinking
winter was gone. You heard one crow's call claw
across the sky and thought he'd dragged back spring.
He'd been there all along. It was just a thaw.
It fooled me too—that icicle outside
our bedroom was losing its pelvic flare,
thinning to a thigh, slowly sliding
down itself in the sun as we walked out there.
Remember our white-haired neighbors? Her stiff
small steps made us laugh. She couldn't see the ice
was gone. She gripped that old husband as if
he might disappear. Now feel the tightness
of my arm around you. Don't you dare go.
You've got to help me through this boot-knocked snow.

Granny Dunn Says Go Back

"Don't get old. When you get to a certain point just turn around and go back."

Granny Dunn

Sometimes her tongue is numb
all morning, she says, but
she doesn't say when
to go back, maybe at the first
crackle of bone as you bend
for the baby's dropped spoon.
Granny waves her own words
away, *Go back,* she beats
the blood back into her fingertips,
waves me off the porch but
doesn't say where to go, back
to a body as supple
as a ballet dancer's, back to stretch
slowly open, spring, summer,
like a time-lapse tulip,
back to a sigh touching
down deep in a lover's chest
before a husband grows
into the shade of a thick
tree where he sits and waits
for his breath. Granny's husband
is gone but she never says how
to go back with your back

turned against the old widow
who waits for you on the porch
of your last house, not wanting
to let it go, go back
before the sun makes her
dizzy in spring, in summer,
before her hip crumbles
against the steps, back to where
she is young with someone
to hold her hips
in his hands, but no
son, no grandson, no one
coming to scoop her up
with tall smiles and carry her
away.

Lula Mae Joins the Procession

I remember my father's freshly lacquered Ford.
I was sitting inside it with Lida
at the wheel, two sisters taking our first
ride without our father, in 1924.

I saw a gentleman tip his hat in the sun,
but not at us. I looked around and saw
what we must do, pull off the road
and let that funeral pass. I knew

we should have stopped and bowed
our heads and waited there in a powder
of pink clay-dust by the pecan grove.
But we drove on. What was it

that happened? My sister's fingers fumbled
at the wheel and we found ourselves rolling
slowly among the mourners, the numb ones,
down the road to a stranger's grave.

Soon we were at the gate. How could we
turn back? Two hatless, gloveless girls,
we bit down our laughter right there
among the black gloves and gardenias,

but then a prickling in my forehead
and then we were both weeping for someone
else's mother or daughter or sister.
Who could we ever tell?

Not my father with his stern knees
waiting in the parlor. Not Mother
looking up from her lane cake, letting
us lick the lemony sweet glaze.

So sixty years ago I took my secret
to the four-poster cherry bed
where Lida and I lay with our heads together,
laughing until she slept. How long

did I lie there awake? Maybe a window
was open and a honeysuckle breeze breathed
across my throat. Maybe one cricket
was letting go of one

of many many-petalled notes.

After a Long Illness

Damp air breathes against the small of her back.
She pulls her shoulders up, her body slack
as if from sleep that won't wear off. The doctor
said her blood's bloomed back. But it shocks her—
to be touched by air, to smell the ground-up spice
rain has pounded out of the ground. No more ice
anywhere. But she walks as if there were,
or as if she's in that winter room of hers
tiptoeing to the window to pull down dusk
and bury herself deep in her own musk.
If her thoughts go back there now, she must shut
them out, let the crocus come, tulips cut
their colors into the air, let everything—
even the barest, thinnest trees—spider toward spring.

For Roxeanna in Winter

I grew up in the cold, met you in the hot
heart of the South. Pink camellia petals
went limp, loosened all winter but would not
let go. I shook some free, watched them settle
in your hair, then slowly brushed them off.
Your shoulders were peach-butter brown. I touched
each one, stroking your hair into a soft,
loose, lacy braid which tumbled open, rushed
down into my hands. I'd like to go back.
But I stand here boot-deep in northern snow.
I lean to kick this shovel down toward packed
and frozen ground. Somewhere under there I know
such flowers wait to bud and breathe and shout
their colors. I've got to dig them out.

Elizabeth

Oakwood Terrace Nursing Home

Sister

Crescents of lipstick on their coffee cups.
The kitchen was empty, we tiptoed in.
Mother had called them *childless,* said we must
not ask them why—Aunt Helen, Lillian.
We sipped their sugary dregs, our heads tipped
back. Suddenly the clatter of your laugh—
my mouth touched pink—I licked it, rubbed my lips
with my knuckles but couldn't get it off.

Many summers later your daughter tugged
me into your yard, made me spin her, fall
with her into the blurry grass and hug
and hug her there. *Time for coffee,* you called.
Her soft, damp kisses chirped against my face.
Childless. My coffee cup clicked into place.

Daughter

Father never forgave me for the clove
I nudged between his teeth. I made him bite
on it, suck lemon so the doctor might
not smell his breath and reason why he dove
down the stairs instead of walking down them.

The doctor was discreet. When Father moaned
he paused to touch his hand. *A painful bone
to break, sir. You must be patient. Now then.
Your daughter here will take good care of you.*
What a rare summer day—Father asleep
all afternoon. But how long could I keep
him there like that? How long before I flew
from my bed at midnight, pierced by the sound
of birds and, from my window, saw him swing
his cane at a shrub, then circling wings
above his head. He'd find the porch and pound
his way in. One night, a delicate knock
at the door. Father! He looked right at me.
A stranger's look, a feigned sobriety,
I thought, and smiled. But then the shock—
He sat down: *Lizzie, I've had a stroke.*
His eyelid, his lip slipping down. This joke
had gone too far. Stop it, Father.

Wind

Today he came, the boy I call Father.
I've had in mind to ask why he bothers.

He said the air smelled creamy with the last
of the roses. Then it happened so fast—

I told him *Yes.* He helped two nurses load
me into the wheelchair. I had to hold

on tight as I rolled out into the bright,
blowing sun. I closed my eyes. What a sight

I was! I remembered how once I crushed
an old cicada. Dry sparks of sound rushed

out, drizzled down. Late August, early fall,
my mind skidding on leaves. He pushed me all

the way into the garden, my hair wild
by then, white webs across my cheek. A child

was staring at me. A slow explosion
of petals rose on the wind. The notion

to ask him filled me: I wanted to know
why God makes me stay here. Why can't I go

with Him? Wind lifted my hair. Father James
smoothed it down. My tongue thickened. All the names

of things were wrong. I meant *soul* but said *heart.*
The wind kept tearing all my words apart.